RHYTHM and POETRY

by
KARL NOVA

All poems © Karl Nova
Illustrations by Joseph Witchall

ISBN : 978-0-9954885-4-0

First published in 2017
by Caboodle Books

A Catalogue record for this book is available from the British Library.
Page Layout by Highlight Type Bureau Ltd, Leeds LS20 8LQ
Printed and bound by CPI Group (UK) Ltd, Croydon, CR0 4YY

The paper and board used in this book are natural recyclable products made
from wood grown in sustainable forests. The manufacturing processes
conform to the environmental regulations of the country of origin.

Caboodle Books Ltd.
Riversdale, 8 Rivock Avenue,
Steeton, BD20 6SA, UK.

Contents

Introduction

I never thought I would be doing this but I am actually writing this to welcome you to my first book ever. I am thankful to you for taking time to read this. I discovered the power of words very early. I am thankful to my mother for introducing me to books as a child. I have lots of memories of these words I read from books she bought for me painting pictures in my young and very active imagination. They transported to me to new worlds and different universes as I turned each page.

I am thankful to my older cousin for playing me the first Hip Hop I ever heard in my life when I was 7 years old. I am glad that the very first MC I ever heard was the legendary Rakim. That was a defining moment in my life. I found a poetic language that spoke directly to me. Fast forward to the present and I am now an artist myself that participates in the culture and art form of stitching and weaving words together to tell my own story.

I am thankful for the day that I first heard the amazing Saul Williams in his movie "SLAM". A particular scene where he performed a spoken word piece in a prison yard totally blew my mind. When I saw that I knew I had to do this. I just had to. I was that skinny kid that felt he had no power but suddenly I realised I had words which were the most powerful things in the world and freely at my disposal!

I am thankful for good teachers. I had a teacher in primary school read my essay to the whole class. He felt what I wrote was the best example of how an essay should be written. I was only 10 years old and the essay topic we were given was to describe ourselves. It was a very special moment to have my words being read out loud. I never thought that would happen but it seems my words or the way I put them together was something my dear teacher felt worthy of being heard. That's what it is all about, being heard.

I use poetry to say what is hard to say any other way. I use poetry to make sense of all the thoughts in my head and feelings in my chest. I use poetry to capture moments like when I take photographs, when I perform them it is like I am taking out pictures from my phone and showing them to you. So let's have a look at some lyrical pictures.

This book contains verses I perform when I do workshops in schools as well as elsewhere. I feel like I am talking to a younger me mainly in this collection. Since it is my first book I think that is a good place to start. It also contains little stories behind each piece. I called this collection rhythm and poetry which is an acronym for rap. Rap music is where my appreciation for poetry started. That love took me to spoken word poets and all kinds of writers from Shakespeare to Maya Angelou, from William Wordsworth to Linton Kwesi Johnson. I hope these words transport you on a journey through my heart and mind. I hope they uplift, inform and inspire.

Poetry?

When I was a kid
poetry seemed boring
complex words on a page
that almost left me snoring
I felt no connection
the language seemed foreign
if it fought for my attention
it was pointless warring
I was introduced to texts
held in high esteem
I did recognise the genius
but they meant nothing to me
all that changed
when I heard an M.C
speak a poetic language
that really hit deep
it's like I woke up
from being fast asleep
everything seemed to slow down
I felt my soul leap
I was amazed
how his words transformed him
from being a skinny geek
into someone enormous
He gained energy
as he kept performing
Something was awakened in me
that was dormant
it deeply moved me
to pick up a pen
and put down lines of my own

lots of gems
I discovered, buried deep in my soul
I dug deeper
struck oil and found gold
now I share all these riches
that I've found
communicating feelings and thoughts
through sound
now that's poetry I'm glad
that I've found
the kind that speaks to me
right here and right now.

Whenever I go to schools to perform and do workshops, I ask the young people if they like poetry and the answer is normally no. When I ask if they like rap, the answer is normally yes. When I show them that rap is actually an acronym for rhythm and poetry and a form of poetry it leaves most of them surprised. This just tells me that the idea of what poetry is needs to be examined. William Shakespeare is great and normally his name comes to mind when poetry is mentioned but the "poets" that a lot of young people identify with today are rappers. I can identify with that because that is my story. Many will argue that a lot of the "poetry" of popular rappers is mostly negative, vulgar and low in quality but at its best rap is one of the highest forms of poetry and it is the voice of this generation. You can't escape rap today. Young people are immersed in it. Rap employs all the literary devices and figures of speech that great men like Shakespeare used. I use these facts to communicate to tell anyone and everyone that rap is poetry and in its highest form, it is great literature.

My address

You will find me on rhythm and poetry street
where lyricism, poetic lines and the spoken word meet
the lines are blurry here it's hard to trace
but for me it is home a familiar place
It is all art you must know this from the start
for me it's a blazing dart I use to pierce the dark
when I move my lips and speak I move hearts
I reach for the sky, sharp like the London Shard
In conversations I'm soft-spoken, very calm
but I speak with strength when the mic is in my palm
from the opening bars I pour out my soul
and fill up empty spaces, freely I flow
though these words I spew and energy I exude
by some won't be viewed as art, what I do
is write my life and speak on the mic
I embody the body of work I recite

One of the things rappers/MCs love to do is write and rap about rapping. I have really thought about why we do this. I think it is because we're normally speaking from a first person point of view and we want to paint a picture of who we are. I know some people make fun of rappers that do that a lot but I don't care, I love it. It helps you understand how much we love this art form. I live and breathe this art every day of my life

Waiting for that bell to ring

I know school is important and a place I have to go
I know I have a lot to learn, there's a lot I don't know
But it's been a long day and I did a lot of things
Now I'm waiting for that bell to ring

When it gets to the final moments of the day
time seems to slow down, the end seems further away
It doesn't always feel like this
the clock I'm watching
while waiting for that bell to ring

I look around the class I'm sure we all feel the same
Silently counting down it's like a secret game
We're like birds ready to flap our wings
We're just waiting for that bell to ring

I appreciate my teachers their job must be hard
Keeping up with every one of us they are in charge
We can be a lot of work, I'm sure it's draining
I bet they're waiting for that bell to ring

I can remember being in school and it would get to the last 30 minutes of the day. I can remember myself watching the clock and just wishing I could press a fast forward button so that the final bell of the day would ring sooner. Unfortunately there isn't any button like that so I just had to wait like everyone else. It was only when I grew up that I thought "I bet the teachers felt the same way we students did"

Homework

I really want to do my homework
but I am so distracted
I mean how can I do it
I'm being honest the fact is
I'd rather be on Facebook
Or chatting on whatsapp
then scroll through Instagram
or spend time on snapchat

I want to watch videos on YouTube
or FaceTime with my friend
A call is coming through on Skype
a text message I have to send
I've got a game to play on Xbox
I've almost reached the end
My favourite show is on TV
I don't want to miss it again

So did I do my homework?
I'll let you take a guess
my answer for you now
is neither no nor yes
the questions you should answer
the ones that need reaction
is have YOU done YOUR homework?
and what are YOUR distractions?

When I was growing up, I had video games and TV to distract me. I also had comics that I loved a lot. I can only imagine how it is to be young and in school now and have more distractions like Youtube, Twitter, Facebook, Snapchat, Instagram, skype, Whatsapp etc etc as well as video games, TV and comics too. I wonder if I would have ever gotten my homework done. My parents would have been extra strict and watchful. I always tell the story of how I not only had to do homework from school but I also had a father who would give me extra homework. Occasionally, he would tell me to write essays or try to get me to read books that I felt were too complex for me. In addition to that, I had a tutor who would come to our house to give me extra lessons! That would also mean extra homework!

Headphones

Opened my eyes, hopped out of bed and brushed my teeth
I had a shower, had some breakfast, let's hit the streets
Yesterday I had a fresh haircut, I'm lined up
My mind feels razor sharp, I saw the clock
It had just struck nine, I knew it was time
I put my phone and my wallet in my pocket, stepped outside
I made sure I locked the front door
I took a breath of fresh air looked around and saw
that though it was the weekend, people were around
they were out and about but that is city life no doubt
I hit my stride as I walked down the street
I had walked for five minutes then it hit me

I forgot my headphones at home!
I can't move around without my music! Oh no!
I retraced my steps and hurried back to my flat
because me without music is like a train with no tracks
with my headphones on I feel like I'm in a movie
the music is the soundtrack that moves me
I stepped outside again I smiled with satisfaction
I pressed play and started walking,
lights! Camera! Action!

I can't even say how many times this has happened to me. In fact there are times I am so far from home that I don't have time to go back and get my headphones. I love music, I need it every day as I travel around. I create music so I always have it on everywhere I am. It makes me feel like my life is a film and every good film needs a soundtrack.

The Dancer

From a distance all I could see
was a crowd gathered round
I could also hear the music
and I really loved the sound

It was a sunny summer afternoon
and as I moved closer
It's like the heat increased,
I was sipping on a cola
I pushed to the front of the crowd
and what I saw
was so amazing
that it left me in awe
a man in a red tracksuit
was spinning on the floor
He was spinning on his head
then suddenly he paused
He twisted his arms and legs to the rhythm
He was popping and locking
to beats from a sound system
The crowd roared at every move,
he danced rapidly
He did things that made me think
he could defy gravity
He did back flips and front flips, so acrobatic
all In time with the beat, so fantastic
"He's so flexible his joints must be elastic"
Is what I thought to myself as the music blasted.

I remember my first visit to New York City. I was amazed the whole time I was out there. I went to perform at a concert and also do some sightseeing. I was at the entrance of Brooklyn Bridge subway station about to get on a train when I saw a man breakdancing on the street. I had never seen anyone dance the way he did, it was amazing. Breakdancing is one of the elements of Hip Hop which was birthed in New York City, it is definitely poetry in motion.

The Chase

Woke up in the morning and I felt so good
went for a walk in my neighbourhood
I thought to myself "I'll go see my friend"
looked at my watch it was quarter past 10
I knew it was early but it was the weekend
So I pulled out my phone, a text I decided to send
He sent me one back saying "cool, see you later"
I just knew this good day would be greater
I got to his house and opened up his front gate
what I saw made my heart to race
with a vicious looking dog I was face to face
My feet followed my heart with a quick pace
I ran and I ran and while running I looked back
This dog was chasing me like we were running track
In my life I never knew I could run this fast
I felt like flash or like lightening as I dashed
this all happened in a few seconds
but it felt like forever, though the time I wasn't checking
I escaped, I was soaking with sweat
I kept wondering when did my friend get a new pet?

This poem was inspired by being chased by a dog when I went over to a friend's house when I was really young. I can still remember the fear I had while I was being chased by that mad dog. Sometimes I think maybe if I didn't run immediately the dog wouldn't have chased me but I wasn't ready to take the risk of finding out if that theory was true.

The Puddle

Voices echoed across the playground
until it all sounded muddled
everyone was playing and running around
and there I was staring into a puddle

I can't remember why I was staring
maybe because it was so dirty
I was just a kid and not caring
that I was close to something so murky

It all happened suddenly I was stunned
It felt like someone pushed fast forward
there was no warning I couldn't run
I got pushed into the puddle, how awkward

Face down in the puddle, dirty and wet
I'm glad my teacher came to get me out
Cold and shivering, I was upset
Thankfully some dry clothes for me were found

I never discovered who pushed me in
for a long time I wondered I was puzzled
my short tale might make you grin
all I'll say is don't stand too close to puddles

This poem is actually based on a true story. This is exactly what happened to me when I was about 7 years old. It happened so quickly but I never forgot this and I really did wonder for a long time who pushed me in. I never found out who did it!

Action Replay

I've always wanted to try this
so let me begin
I want to tell a story in reverse
let's start from the end
The ball jumps out
of the back of the net
back to the tip of the boot
of the striker as he stretched

The clock goes backwards from being just seconds left
from this cup final ending 3 - 3
the crowd is tense
The striker wearing number 9
runs backwards past 3 players
of the opposing team
the ball cuts back like a razor
to the centre circle
where his team had kicked off
after the opposing team
had equalised to 3 all
The ball goes back
into the hand of the striker
he goes back in reverse
and puts the ball in his net
because what had happened was
he had scored an own goal
In the last minute of extra time
with seconds left

One of my favourite rappers of all time, Nas has a song called
"Rewind" where he tells a full story backwards and I have always
wanted to try telling a story of my own in that way. This short poem
is my attempt at it. The title is also a play on the idea of rewinding
something you are watching so that you can watch it again. Back in
the day before DVDs and watching things online, VHS tapes and video
players were what people mainly used. You could hold rewind on the
remote control if you were watching a tape and you would see
everything go backwards in reverse. You can do the same thing today
with sky TV for example and rewind live TV.

Animal Talk

Once upon a rhyme is how I want to start this
story that's being told by this artist
I must've been asleep, this must've been a dream
because a dog walked up and started talking to me
It said "I'm man's best friend and you look like you need one"
I couldn't even respond because I was so stunned
The dog said, "what's the matter, cat got your tongue?
You look like a cool cat.." and as the dog spoke on

A chicken crossed the road as it did it spoke
It said "I'm sure you wanna know why, like that old joke"
When the chicken said that I heard hyenas laughing
I looked to my left and saw a few of them passing
A sly fox appeared and said to the dog,
"Are you really man's best friend? that's so odd"
A sharped eyed eagle hovered above
It was chatting with a hawk, a seagull and a dove

All this while I didn't say a word
I was shocked at everything I'd seen and heard
So I got up and started walking
the dog followed and kept on talking
we caught up to a tortoise who said
"hey there, I'm in a race with a very fast hare"
we kept moving we came across a zebra, donkey and horse
laughing about how they were cousins of course
I saw pig that was rolling in mud
It smiled and squealed "I know you love bacon, sausages and pork
chops"
We took a break and sat on a log

We saw a frog hopping while sipping on a tea cup
The frog said to the dog "what's up who is this?
I'll be on my way I'm just minding my business"
The dog started chatting to a beaver
who wanted to walk with us but dog was like "you're too eager"

The beaver said, "fine, watch out for the snake, get advice from the wise owl and stay safe,
remember to check the water for sharks before swimming
look for the lion king and don't do any fishing"
We kept moving and saw a monkey, an ape, a chimpanzee and a gorilla
and also an orangutan having dinner
They were like "hey dog what's up how you doing?
And where in the world did you find that human?"
the dog was like "I just found him sitting by the road
he seemed lost and alone far away from home
we're on our way to the lion king
and hope we'll find the wise owl, bye for now"
No time to tell you about the bear,
elephant and tiger we saw on our way there
became I woke from this dream, dazed and confused
and remembered that today I'm going to the zoo!

I once had a dog called Junior when I was a kid that I loved so much. I spent so much time with this dog that I used to have imaginary conversations with it. This piece was just me imagining what it would be like for animals to talk. My dog ran away from home and I never saw it again. Sometimes I wonder, where did Junior go?

Winter fall

It was a cold winter day,
walking down Oxford street
is what I was doing,
I have very quick feet
I was window shopping
going into different shops
I had no care in the world
my jacket was zipped up.
The street was busy
as it normally is
I weaved through the crowd
by countless people I whizzed
What happened next
is kind of hard to explain
It's like the whole world moved and froze,
hear what I'm saying
You see what happened was
somehow I slipped
I fell down face to the floor
my jacket ripped
not every part of it,
only just a bit
I was so stunned
when the ground I hit
It reminded me of when
I was pushed into a puddle
for a few seconds
I was down
on this busy street puzzled

A few nice people
helped me stand up
I was still stunned and embarrassed
I laughed it off
I mumbled my words of thanks
and brushed the dust off
I looked to the ground shocked
thinking to myself "what?!"
I looked around at busy street
to see if anyone watched
then into the nearest shop
I quickly ducked.

When this happened I was not a kid. I was fully grown up unlike when I got pushed in the puddle which I recounted in the poem, "The Puddle". No one pushed me this time. I just simply slipped and missed my step. I am really thankful for the helpful people that came to my aid. London is a busy city and people hardly have time to stop. I will never forget how I felt. I was so embarrassed that I just had to quickly vanish into the nearest shop.

Younger me

Sometimes I imagine
walking down the street
and by chance
bumping into a younger me
I know it's unlikely
this will happen you see
but for a minute
join me and daydream
I would tell myself
enjoy every moment
live fully in the present
grab it and own it
don't be in a hurry
to become a grown up
It's going to happen anyway
the future is going to show up
I know you love to play
but first do your homework
work hard then play hard
put first things first
Respect your elders
because one day you'll be one
listen twice as much as you speak
you have one tongue
and two ears
this will make more sense
as you gain years
always be curious
ask questions
you'll always be a student of life
learning lessons

Dream big
use your imagination
just like how you're imagining
this situation
of me bumping into
my younger self
I know it's not gonna happen
so listen and listen well

I love movies about time travel. Imagine if it were really possible to go back in time. This piece was inspired by my fascination with the idea of time travel. You learn more as time goes on and It would be amazing to be able to go back in time and talk to a younger you and share some of the things you have learnt that you didn't know before. You might even be able to stop something bad from happening if it was possible to go back in time. Since it isn't possible, all we can do is imagine.

Four seasons

Summer is the best time
so let me start right here
It's my favourite season
I wish it could last all year
The sun feels real near
and it can get so hot
which funnily leads to
some people complaining a lot

After that comes Autumn
some call it the fall
because the leaves change colour
and fall, covering the ground like a shawl
The temperature is cooler
Most times you'll need a light jacket
The holiday is over and back to school
go the students to their classes

Winter sneaks up on you
you start to feel the chill
the festive season approaches
anticipation builds
The Christmas lights come on
The big day arrives
We countdown to the new year
The nights are cold like ice

Spring appears on the horizon
after short dark days and long nights
Jack Frost loses his icy grip
The flowers come out, a beautiful sight
Holiday ends, students back in school again
The excitement of the new year fades
as the months go on it gets warmer
summer returns again with heat waves

I wrote this poem in winter which is my least favourite season in the year. I do love Christmas and New Year celebrations but I wish we could skip the cold bit totally. Here in the UK we love to complain about not having great summers but the truth is I prefer any kind of summer we get to winter. We Londoners love complaining, I bet if we had a perfect summer we would complain it is too perfect!

Peer Pressure

The fear of being left out is what it is all about
No one wants to get laughed at or be the odd one out
No one likes to feel rejected put down and dejected
we all love to feel accepted, we're all affected
but you have to learn to be your own person
just be yourself and aim to be your best version
You're not a robot programmed to follow without thinking
just acting brainless with empty eyes blinking
I understand the pressure it doesn't stop as you grow
It's natural to follow where everybody goes
and sometimes it's ok to go with the flow
but other times you have to swim against the tide and so
you'll have to say no, when everyone say yes
and be firm with your choice deep in your chest
and overcome that fear of being left out
because that's what peer pressure is really all about

This piece is pretty straightforward. I remember when I was younger I wanted to be so badly accepted by the cool kids in my area. I went out of my way to do things I knew I shouldn't do just to be accepted by them. I later realised I didn't have to do that to be cool. Being myself and thinking for myself and even choosing to do things that were sometimes opposite to what everyone was doing made me stand out. It got people wondering "why is he doing something else?" It is not always easy but you have to learn to be yourself and as simple as it sounds sometimes it is a pretty hard thing to do. Peer pressure isn't just a problem young people face. It doesn't matter what age you are, you can feel influenced and pressured to do what everyone else is doing just because it seems like the thing to do to be accepted.

Text message from the future

They're going to tell you it's corny
to dream of a better tomorrow
don't believe them
just leave them alone
and continue along the road
You will hear them say
"Don't be naive, don't be simple minded,
Open your eyes and don't be blinded"
simply because they're tired with heavy eyelids
weighed down by the cares of this world
I know it sounds farfetched
but a time will come
when dreaming big and believing in possibilities
will appear dumb
not to everyone but to some
I mean those who are grumpy
with a mood so glum
Take these words
as a message from the future
a poetic text message
to wake you up and shake you up
Never stop dreaming,
never stop believing
that you can do better
as you keep breathing

**This is a poem that goes with "Younger me" but from another angle.
Imagine if you got a text message from the future from...............
yourself! Ok so I know that is a bit of a farfetched concept and will
never happen in real life but just imagine what that would be like! It**

is hard to explain to young people that as you grow up it can sometimes become harder to believe in possibilities but in some cases this is true. If I could, I would definitely text younger me and tell myself that I should never stop dreaming, believing and working hard to make those dreams come true.

Words

Everyday doing dumb things
on their smartphones
It could be a him or a her
using their words to hurt
every other line is a curse
grabbing for attention
for a response they search
keyboard warriors love to start a war
these hungry trolls are starving for more
Maybe they're angry or just bored
the goal is a reaction
they want to score
they say to themselves
it's only harmless banter
but sometimes things said
are more deadly than terminal cancer
words have power,
watch what you say
whether you type them online
or speak them, they carry weight
but wait
maybe you don't really care
about the thoughts and feelings you put in the air
one day you'll realise words are like seeds
and when planted you will reap deeds
words have power,
watch what you say
whether you type them online
Or speak them they carry weight
but wait
You really should care
about the thoughts and feelings you put in the air

Words are powerful. Just think of how you use words during your day. You talk to people, you crack jokes, you get information, you give information, words are so important. To further highlight the importance of words, just imagine if you had no words at all. Life would definitely be different. I wrote this poem thinking about the power of words and in the times we are currently in where we are all on things like twitter, facebook, snapchat etc I think people are realising the power of their words even more. A lot of times we can use words negatively instead of positively. I wrote this piece thinking about how words can be misused because we forget how powerful they are.

Student of life

As a student I dreamt of the day
When the phase of school days would be far away
I used to daydream all day everyday
my imagination grew wings, my mind did migrate
Thankfully this didn't affect my grades
because my brain was sharp like a razor blade
I did my homework and got lots of As
but couldn't wait until the holidays
I used to wonder
 "why do I have to come here?"
Then I remembered my parent's voice in my ear
"You have to go to school to get a job or career"
only later would I understand their concerns and fears
All I wanted was to play with my mates
But "life isn't a game" is what my elders would say
I'm no more in school but I'm still a student
life is my main teacher now
Sometimes I'm learning with bemusement

I remember when I was in primary school. I used to imagine the day I would never ever have to go to school again. It seemed so far away in the future. The day finally came when I realised that I didn't have to be in school again! As time went on I found myself missing school days and I could not believe I was feeling that way. If you had told me "Karl you are going to miss school times one day" back when I was in primary/secondary school, I would have never agreed. The funny thing is even after you leave University you never really leave "school" life becomes your main teacher. I came to the realisation that I am a student of life for life.

Stating The Obvious

I used to hate when people state the obvious
like someone saying that water is wet
or the grass is green
or the sky is blue
or not everything you read is true on the Internet
Isn't it obvious we should all say thank you, sorry and please?
and we should speak words that we really mean?
Maybe we do need reminders
because some people get crueller instead of kinder.
My mama knows I love her
but she likes to hear me say it when I hug her
obviously it's right to be polite
but how come so many are rude most times?
the best place to hide something is in plain sight
because sometimes we miss things
right before our eyes
it's like the story of the Emperor's new clothes
it took a child to say the truth that everyone
should have known
I guess we do need to state the obvious
obviously many find this preposterous

Imagine if you had a friend that told you one day "Hey guys, the grass is green, the sky is blue and water is wet" as if he or she was saying something no one ever heard before? That is how I feel when sometimes when people say stuff that is so obvious that everyone should know already. The thing is just because certain things are common knowledge it doesn't mean you can't overlook them. Sometimes you need reminders of things that are viewed as so obvious it's silly repeating them. Even writing this poem was stating the obvious about stating the obvious.

You've gotta love it

You have to learn to love learning
because every day as the world is turning
yes the very earth you stand on is spinning
the times are changing and shifting
and if you don't take time to listen
so many things you'll be missing

So you have to love learning
the fire of curiosity
in you must keep on burning
because whether you like it or not
You're a student of life for life
and things in life will test you
so I guess you have no choice
you have to press through

You have to love learning
keep yearning for knowledge, you need to keep searching
make wisdom and understanding your best friends
Think of them like a warm and loving uncle or aunt
sharing stories with truth in them

You have to love learning
Even when it is hard,
leaving your belly churning
remember there are different ways to
some of them will amaze you
others might dismay you
and even if I can't persuade you
I hope we can learn to love learning
and be grateful

I love learning new things but sometimes learning is tough and scary. I have always been a curious kind of person and this has led to me digging up and discovering things I probably wouldn't have bothered to know about if I didn't keep my curiosity. Never lose that. Always be curious, always ask questions. That's one of the ways to keep learning and to love it as well.

I'm gonna make it

Don't let anyone ever tell you, you cannot make it
dream big success is there for you to take it
certain people you see, all they do is fake it
they claim that they've made it,
they claim they're the greatest
but don't watch them, you stay focused
'cause if you lose focus, you will be hopeless
never be afraid to dream or think big
believe in yourself and you will achieve it
just believe it and see yourself reach it
and keep your dreams safe just like a secret
always stay cool when things get heated
and no matter what you won't be defeated
life is like a mission to be completed
with great importance it must be treated
so inhale success deeply breathe it
just like air in your lungs you need it
now say, I'm gonna make it!

Don't let anyone ever tell you, you cannot make it
dream big success is there for you to take it
it is your birthright, I'm speaking of greatness
some lack love for self and that's why there's hatred
don't give in to peer pressure and follow the crowd
you were born to be a leader so learn to walk it out
life is like school so you better learn your lessons
pass your exams 'cause they'll be times you're tested
this message, I send like a text, what's next?

I always tweet, 'cause tweets are the cousins of texts
my Facebook pages are inspirational
the handwriting on the wall is so readable
my face aint poker faced like the lady
who's got the world going gaga like a baby
my expression is clear for you to see and hear
and like a cotton bud I will clear out your ear saying
I'm gonna make it!

Don't let anyone ever tell you, you cannot make it
dream big success is there for you to take it
success is sweet, I know you like to taste it
it tastes better than MCd's or Nandos that's basic
sometimes you might fall short like a dwarf
or a midget but after that stand tall
people might laugh at you and say that you're silly
but don't pay attention them when they're chilly
giving you the cold shoulder they try to hurt you
and sometimes friends yeah, they might desert you
when that happens just brush your shoulders off
keep your head up and square your shoulders up
and no matter what happens or what people say
you were born to be somebody, born to be great
you are whatever you think in your heart
so shine bright like the star that you are and say,
I'm gonna make it!

When I first started visiting schools to do workshops, this piece was the first thing I wrote. It represents the main message I have for young people. I originally called it "letter to a younger me" and eventually set it to music, so now it is actually a song! It wasn't my intention at first to make a song out of these verses. It is all about aspirations and motivating yourself to achieve your goals. You have to believe in yourself and work hard to achieve the results you want. When I visit a school or even perform on stage at a concert, I would love to end up motivating and inspiring people to believe and achieve against all odds and in spite of difficulties. I use this piece to motivate myself because there are many goals I haven't achieved yet!

True Colours

It's not always black or white
sometimes there's grey area
this makes some folks blue
and feel life is scarier
I don't mind grey area
'cause see I am colourful
not just because of my brown skin so wonderful
I was sippin' orange juice
watching the colour purple
the sun hung in the sky like a gold circle
this is a stolen moment, call me a bandit
you've caught me in the act
you've caught me red handed
I was contemplating on how I can make some green
when a song from pink
came on my tv screen
my mind drifted
I thought of the indigo O2
when I was at an award show
and trouble brewed
violence broke out
by a crowd I was swept
into a female loo
with a blonde and brunette
their faces were pale
and they were scared to death
but my thoughts were crystal clear
as I held my breath
I escaped and I saw some crimson splashes
on the shirt of a guy

who had caught some slashes
so many things are fake
like false eyelashes
but I see your true colours
in glimpses and flashes

This piece was inspired by a piece by my friend and mentor Breis called "The Colourful Return" He basically used a lot of colours to tell a story. I decided to do the same thing and what I wrote is based on a true story. I always tell it when I visit schools.

I was at an award show at the indigo2 which is at the O2 arena and was nominated for some music I did with a group I was in at the time. A fight broke out and there was a stampede. I ran out of the venue with many others then went back in because we thought security had it all under control. The night went on and everything was back to normal but then all of a sudden I heard a loud shattering sound of a bottle breaking and all hell broke loose. Another stampede happened and I tried to head to the exit. I found myself being pushed in another direction by the crowd and ended up in the female toilet! There were many other people both guys and girls hiding there already.

I decided to get into a cubicle to feel safer so I kicked open the door of nearest cubicle. There were 2 ladies hiding there, one was blonde and the other brunette. They were so scared and thought I was involved in the fighting. After assuring them I wasn't I hid for a few minutes then I decided to take a chance and get out of there. I left the toilet and got into the main hall where fighting was still happening and ran out of the main exit. In the foyer I saw someone lying unconscious and another person bleeding. I made it out the exit and ran as fast I could to the nearest underground train station (North Greenwich)

When I got home I switched on the news while still being in shock and a report of what happened came on. Thankfully no one died. I wrote this piece afterwards. I realised that fame, glitz and glamour wasn't all that I thought it was and recommitted to always be positive and never promote violence in anything I do.

No Beef

I'm sealing this with no flaws
I'm in the room for improvement, no doors
walk through the corridors of my mind
no stairs for you to climb because I am blind
blind to the hateful stares, I take lifts
I'm going straight to the top it takes patience
it's that escalator flow, yeah I'm rising
like the sun at dawn on the horizon
I'm not in the hall of fame,
more like the hall of shame
I'm now in the hall of faith
my mind changed
I'm in this for the long haul,
walk with me
they say the walls have ears,
will they talk with me?
the handwriting is on the wall I read it
I fill in the blanks with words of thanks
there's so much hate
but I won't feed it
I don't do beef
so with peace I leave it

Now just because I don't do beef
don't call me chicken
I know what's at steak
I don't lack liver, listen
revenge is never satisfied, it eats you up
it has an appetite for destruction and thus
when it comes to that, I would rather starve

than feed into the hype of trying to be hard
when I was young I wanted to scrape the plate
but retaliation leaves a bitter aftertaste
he has a chip on his shoulder
it seems they all do
so many chips, I'm sure ketchup will spill soon
and all the tears in the world
won't wash it away
somehow it seems to leave, permanent stains
too much fast food is not healthy for you
it can clog your heart,
so watch what you chew
they say you are what you eat
that's why I don't beef
but I'm not a vegetarian I love meat

How many more tears have got to drop?
or does your heartbeat have to stop?
does it have to get six feet deep
before you wake up from your deep sleep?
trust me it's deep
and deep inside you know
you've been wounded deep inside your soul
in fact I take it back because you don't know
you've been blinded and that's why the guns blow
So that's me in the sun walking
I'm hearing these guns talking
MCs echo the gun talk of the streets
and guess what?
we see more blood pouring
oh you think you're a man now
because you have a gun now,
because you have a knife now?
the truth is you feel powerless

and you're the definition of what a coward is
without your guns who are you?
without your knives who are you?
without your crew who are you?
I have no beef
I am through

The way I wrote this piece was so weird. I woke up one morning from having a dream where I was rapping. I was just coming up with lines off the top of my head in my dream and the first two lines of this piece were the lines I woke up with. I actually woke up saying them!! This piece ended up being about how I want to promote peace. We all know what beef is. I don't mean the kind that comes from cows. Beef is just slang for when you have a grudge or contention with someone. After seeing what beef taken to the extreme can do, I decided I wanted to be someone that spreads peace and positivity. I don't want beef.

Boys in the woods

I've seen those tough as oaks
weep like willows
even the hardest thugs can have tear stained pillows
most can't see the forest for the trees
because they're so up close and in too deep,
it leaves them with a perception
that can't see the bigger picture
and sticking to their point of view
becomes the main fixture
Sometimes taking step back
gives a broader view
so take a step back, pause
and think things through
now don't stay rooted
when it's time to move
there's a time to branch out
after which you'll see fruit
I saw a tree stand tall
with its green crown
it looked like a million axes
couldn't bring it down
I leaned against its trunk
like on the shoulder of a friend
you know those tried and tested ones
on them alone you can depend
they can shield you from the rain
and cool you off when it's hot
they will back you up
when against a wall you're backed up
Yes life can get hard like the hardest tree bark
Don't get lost in the woods
when it's late and it's dark

I love trees. I remember as a kid climbing trees all the time. My friends and I thought we were heroes because we could climb trees so easily. When I think of trees I also think of long walks in the woods. I remember as a child I went for a long walk without telling anyone and by the time I got home, police had been called to search for me. When I was told that walking in the woods alone is dangerous for a 7 year old, I couldn't understand the fuss because I felt no fear at all. I felt like the trees could protect me and cover me. When I think of trees, I think of friends and loved ones that are dependable and always there for me.

For Not Against

I once heard something wise
it made a lot of sense
"make sure you're defined by what you're for
rather than what you're against"
So I sat and I thought
what am I really for?
it was like in my mind
I opened a huge door
I'm for love, I'm for peace
I'm for joy, I'm for good times
I'm for great conversation
where we dialogue and rub minds
I'm for wisdom, I'm for intelligence,
I'm for knowledge, understanding
I'm for excellence
I'm for respect both of self and for others
I'm for learning new things
there's a lot to discover
I'm for dreaming big with a vivid imagination
I'm for believing in a bright future
that's my destination
I'm for good food and good music
I'm not a great cook
but music, I produce it
I'm for good books
I'm for spreading truth and light
I'm for doing good and right
even though sometimes I fight
to stay on the right path
I'm for guidance and direction

I'm for a good laugh
and also quiet reflection
I'm for showing loved ones affection
I'm for respecting my elders
and encouraging the youth
I'm for drinking clean water
and also fresh fruit juice
I'm for justice and equality for all
I'm not for calling it soccer
I'm for calling it football
I'm for all things positive
and all things good
I'm for being heard clearly
I'm for being understood
I once heard something wise
it made a lot of sense, it went:
"make sure you're defined by what you're for
rather than what you're against"

We live in a world when it seems to be easier to say what you are against than what you are for, this is why you see people debating online and offline all day every day. With all this in mind, I decided to write a piece about it. I couldn't list every single thing I am for though, that would make for a very long verse but I had fun writing this one. I read a quote somewhere that goes "promote what you love instead of bashing what you hate" So I guess this is me trying to do that.

Rhythm And Poetry

I have a way with words
like William Shakespeare or William Wordsworth
I'm here to make clear
that rap is poetry
when it's done properly
I shape and mould verses like clay in poetry
I aim to stay on beat when I'm rhyming
with perfect timing,
like Big Ben when it's chiming
you can tell a story or share your feelings
or have so much fun
you'll be dancing on the ceiling
ok right there I was exaggerating
trying to create humour with what I'm saying
I can be serious but right there I was playing
different sides of you, you will be displaying
I never knew I could do this
until I tried it
I practised and practised
before I used to hide it
but now whenever I perform I get excited
because passion for poetry gets me ignited

what you're experiencing right now
is rhythm and poetry
I'm a poet with rhythm
also known as an M.C
and an M.C is a master of ceremony
microphone controller
real not phony

when I'm rhyming, I use my imagination
to imagine a nation
caught up in celebration
I'm a student of life
this is freestyle education
I've got ingredients
that makes my poetry amazing
my style is fresh
like new trainers straight out of the box
I think out of the box
I'm blessed down to my socks
I'm flipping words with rhythm
and descriptions have got you tripping
it takes a lot of practice
though talent is God given
pronouns, nouns, similes and metaphors
adjectives, verbs and so much more
is what I use to paint pictures
in your mind
I'm not a painter but an artist
of a different kind

What you're experiencing right now
is street poetry, deep poetry
soon you'll be quoting me
I work lyrical miracles
of me it is typical
as a child I was a creative individual
like Banksy I'm a street artist
peep my graffiti
I make 'em with pens and pads
not spray cans, do you read me?
nowadays I type 'em into my smartphone see
I feel like every day is Christmas

I'm that merry
I used to get stage fright
performing was that scary
now it's all fun
like I'm watching Tom & Jerry
I'm in my own zone when I recite my poems
I'm not a clone on the microphone
my story's my own
I used to feel like the odd one out
but in time it seems this odd one won out
'cause no matter what
all of them chat about
on my own I use my own mind
to think things out

This piece came as a direct result of doing workshops in schools. In fact it became a song while I was freestyling and performing in a school. It explains the kind of poetry that has influenced me the most, the poetry found in rap music. Rap isn't normally perceived as poetry but as I point out all the time R.A.P is an acronym for "Rhythm And Poetry" and I decided to make this the title of this book you are reading right now. Sometimes I perform this with music and sometimes without. I do that to just show that the verses have power and rhythm in themselves.

Sometimes when I say that rap is poetry many people don't make that connection because in their view the rap music that they have heard is vulgar and shallow and it possibly being poetry could not be true. In my opinion it doesn't make it any less poetry than verses from Shakespeare. Rap at its best employs all the literary devices that Shakespeare used and can be truly amazing when just looked at on paper. On the other hand, rap has a leg in music and because of this I can understand why it is not viewed as poetry. I am influenced by rap as well as spoken word slam poetry which is closely related to rap but different.

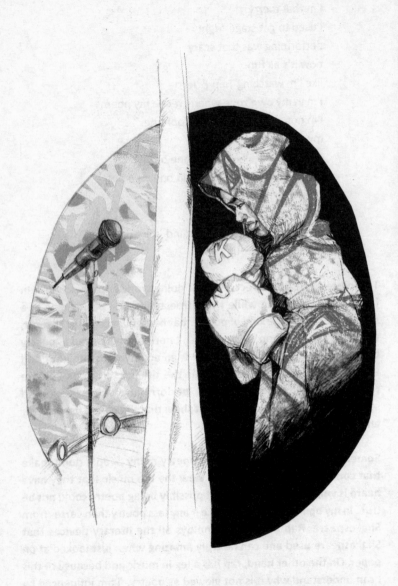

Backstage thoughts

The expectations are rising
in my belly the butterflies are flying
the anticipation is building in the building
and this feeling that I'm feeling is a real thing
I try to act calm like I'm chillin'
but sweat has already started pouring
loudly I can hear the crowd roaring
It's not like it's the first time I'm touring
but the levels this time are so high, soaring
I'm backstage and it's so intense
I've been here before
it doesn't make sense
I start mumbling lyrics under my breath
My heart starts beating louder in my chest
It's like I'm about to box,
I start jogging on the spot
I punch air while shouting what! what!
It's showtime, in no time
I'll be live on the stage
spraying lines
What's this feeling?
is this stage fright?
I know that it will vanish
when I touch the mic
when I clutch the mic
and begin to recite
verses that have substance
not just hype
I'm focused in the zone now
Let's start the countdown

give me the mic now!
10! 9!
it's almost that time
For me to shine with
purpose and design
8! 7!
I'll be on in some seconds
time for kick off,
I'm already sweating
6! 5!
it's gonna be live
Strap on your seat belt
it is time to ride
4! 3!
are you kidding me?
the anticipation's
almost killing me
3! here we go now!
2! here we go now!
1!
It's time to shine bright
like the sun!

I have performed all over the place and in different kinds of settings. I have performed in open air venues like stadiums and festivals and small intimate venues like in clubs. I have even performed in a prison. The feeling of being backstage when I'm about to go on is the same. I hardly feel fear these days but I always have that feeling of anticipation. I decided to write this piece about it to capture that feeling.

I'm Different

When I was young
I was a little troublesome
dreaming I could
blow and pop like bubblegum
before I rapped
my number one fan was my mum
and the only beats I got
were beats on my bum
I was a shy guy
dreaming of being a fly guy
some thought I was a wise guy
I was such a dry guy
up in my room with my stereo
listening to Hip Hop on my radio
back then, my pen, wasn't my best friend
but now we go together like Barbie and Ken
never thought that I would be up on a stage
reciting lyrics that I wrote down on a page
I've been to Europe
also been to America
stood in front of crowds up in Africa
here I am, on the M-I-C
I see that there is much more to me
'cause I've found out the gift of poetry
expressing feelings and thoughts
that belong to me
singing songs and people sing-a-long with me
and there is much more to you
so won't you agree
that
I'm different

I see you weighing me up
wondering if I'm heavy

well I'm ready to rock steady
and make you wiggle like spaghetti
I see your minds ticking
as your eyes are blinking
it's like I can almost hear
what you're thinking
who is this I'm hearing now rapping?
and why does he sound like that
when he's chatting?
is this just another wannabe on the mic?
another wannabe thug who's gassed up and all hype?
why does his flow sound sound like that?
and ummmm why does he jump around like that?
He's even cracking jokes
why does he clown like that?
why did I pay to enter?
give my pounds right back!
I thought he was another wannabe
gangster rapper
I guess I was wrong,
He's more than just swagger
well forget what you heard before
as you are listening
my lines are blistering
'cause see
I'm different

Because of the kind of music I create, how I dress or my physical appearance it is easy for people to try to fit me into a stereotype that is negative. I wrote these verses with the intention to let people know I am different. I want young people to know that they are all unique in their own way and it is ok for them to be themselves. Sometimes it takes guts to just be you because you are different. People are scared of what is different sometimes, it makes them uncomfortable. As long as you are being positive be yourself and be bold.

Writer's Block

The page was empty
I was searching for the words to fill it
I didn't want to write randomly
I wanted to kill it
when I say kill it,
I'm metaphorically speaking
though the pen is mightier than the sword
it is weakened
When you're not on point or sharp with the wordplay
That's like a fencer who is poor with his swordplay
I try to cut to the chase and cut out the clichés
but as you can see doing that isn't easy
When I have writer's block
I write about writing
to get to the voice deep inside me
that is fighting
to be heard clearly and amplified
you have to dig deep to find the gold mine
so I keep digging and looking over what I've written
deep within I feel something that is living
and what is living are my hopes and dreams
the passion for writing
has me bursting at the seams, it seems.
I turn that passion in sentences
those sentences become verses
those verses become poems
that this poet rehearses
and after all the rehearsing
and all of the practising
I find the boldness to share it all
without feeling I'm just rambling

Writing isn't always easy, sometimes you can feel stuck and not know what to write. I wrote my first rap in my early teens, it was a rap about 7Up of all things. I have since then written many poems, songs and rap verses. When I feel inspired writing comes easily but there are times it is hard. Writing this book was a bit scary for me, I kept worrying about whether anyone would be interested. I had to let all of that go and just go with the flow. I had to trust that all the times I have practised writing will help me be able to produce something worth reading.

There is no fixed way a poem should be. If it is a rap verse though, it has to rhyme and you should aim to be creative. You can write about anything you want in any style you like. Just be free. Think outside the box. The aim is to be as creative as you possibly can be. Use your imagination. Express yourself.

I write these poems

I write these poems
To make up for the empty slogans
that gassed me up and left me choking
I held too much in, now outspoken
is how I am, now my mind is open
like a parachute I am floating
I feel light hearted like I'm joking
but the gravity of this situation
is potent

I write these poems
with words carefully chosen
from a heart that once was frozen
but now is thawed out and hoping
that these words will connect
whether they are heard or read
Maybe you'll see what I see
and feel what I feel
and nod your head
Or maybe not

Maybe you won't connect the dots
maybe it won't strike a chord
even though I'm saying a lot
Maybe you can't trace the meaning
and the picture you won't spot
maybe one day it will hit you
and make you suddenly stop
that's fine.

I will keep writing poems
with an unbroken focus
Because these words in my head
demand that they are spoken
I will keep on sketching
In my heart and mind it is etched in
I'm like a mirror, I'm just reflecting
I pour my heart out, it's so refreshing.

I spend a lot of time thinking about poetry (has that been easy to tell so far? hahaha) Sometimes I ask myself "why do I write?" or "what is the purpose of poetry?" There are many reasons why I write. One of the main reasons is to hopefully connect with someone else. I know I have read poetry, or heard spoken word poets perform live and what they have said made me feel like someone else understands what I am feeling and thinking. I know this might sound strange but it can make you feel less lonely. It can be very encouraging. You can even feel inspired and motivated to get through whatever is happening to you.

If I can make someone who reads or hears the verses I write less lonely and like they are understood I feel I have done my job. This is not the only reason why I write but the more I write, I do have it in my mind that someone could read or hear what I am saying and feel some kind of connection.

Lyrical exercise

Yes I'm painting pictures again
not with a paintbrush not with a pen
I type words straight into my phone
Inspiration like oxygen
I breathe in and breathe out
all these verses that I speak out
I'm overflowing they leak out
as I'm out and about
they're floating around
like these clouds
that are over my head
my thoughts are over the edge
it's like I'm at the top of a skyscraper
and I jumped off the ledge
that's just metaphorically speaking
because if it's literal I'd be dead
please don't misunderstand what I've said
break the coded speech instead
My imagination I stretch
It's so elastic
I'm so ecstatic,
I'm blessed
I dream and think bigger than where I'm at, oh yes
I'm exercising my mind,
I'm jogging my memory
my thoughts running through my brain
might leave me a little strained
they say your mind is a muscle
I'm just thinking things through and working it out
I write it all down

to make sense of my thoughts
sometimes I struggle
but I'm writing my vision
and I'm making it plain
What I'm saying is beyond words
It's hard to explain

One thing I like about writing rap verses is how you can just do it for fun without thinking too deep about where you are going to end. I wrote this verse one line after the other as an exercise to see where I could go without any topic in mind. This piece is just a snapshot of what I was thinking and feeling in the moment I wrote it. Writing isn't always about being deep and serious, it can be fun like going for a jog and enjoying the scenery.

Poetry in motion

So many times I've heard them say
think outside the box
that I'm thinking outside the box
of thinking outside the box
thus, I come storming out the block
it's a race against time
I'll break your stopwatch,
if you're clocking me
oh do stop watching me
ok pay attention 'cause the fee is free
actually it's not 'cause time is money
spending time observing is an investment, watch me
they say if you're too serious
you won't chart well
I guess I've got to lighten up
like vybz kartel
I was a class clown, I played that part well
whether I'm laughing or crying
it's heartfelt
I speak flames that makes cold hearts melt
I'm like Guy Fawkes but love makes
my bonfire swell
I was once spellbound
but truth broke my spell
I don't need to spell it out
'cause it aint hard to tell.

I project words from my intellect
to connect and affect you with
positive prospects

I'll help you see clearly
like a guy wearing specs
my verses you digest
both simple and complex
line upon line, I build like an architect
persistence is the blueprint of success
sometimes I talk fast
and almost lose my breath
that's the time I should pause
and maybe take a rest
but I won't stop yet
I've got a lot on my chest
I feel animated like a cartoon regardless
all I really want is to simply do my best
with rhythm and poetry this I confess
I know I will get slated
because to some this is mere entertainment
but it's more than that I think it is blatant
I'm not gonna waste time again
so here we go again

Sometimes my mind bounces from one topic to the next and I like how I sometimes capture this in some verses I write. I feel free when I'm writing, It is all about being in the moment.

When I go to schools to do workshops, I ask the students to give me 10 random words to use to create a freestyle. This is when I just come up with verses off the top of my head in the moment. It is very exciting and challenging.

Don't Feed The Trolls

Don't feed trolls, I say let 'em starve
they are starving for attention
feeding them isn't your job
they're lacking affirmation
and they're seeking validation
can't you see their demonstration?
that is why they're acting odd
keyboard warriors, can't you see they're hungry
they're on the hunt they've got a case of the munchies
with their strawman arguments
be on the lookout because all day they're targeting
anyone
first of all they draw you in
with the bickering if you fall then they win
because they are hiding behind a screen

they've found boldness while they remain unseen
get in touch with your own inner troll
make sure you starve it to keep it under control
ignore rants if they're ignorant
even if the rants are mine are in fact

Don't feed the trolls, most of them are cowards
in person they are soft like the petals of a flower
they wouldn't dare say to your face
what they would type and post online
you know the type I'm not lying
from the safety of their homes
or distance of their phones
they try to set the tone
you must not take the bait
and be hooked into another debate
because all they want is to be noticed
this I've noticed I'm no more a novice
they want to feel like winners
banter to them is breakfast, lunch and dinner
get in touch with your own inner troll
make sure you starve it to keep it under control
ignore rants if they're ignorant
even if the rants are mine are in fact

Sometimes people can be mean when you encounter them online seemingly for no reason. It happens in YouTube comment sections, on Facebook, on twitter, instagram, in blog comment sections etc. Some people are intentionally mean online on purpose. Some people seem to only feel good about themselves when they put down other people. I think people do things like that for the attention it brings them. It seems to make them feel strong. Maybe they are dealing with negative things inside of themselves and because of that they lash out at others from the safety of being behind their screens. This means not giving attention to online trolls could be the worst thing that you can do to them. In some cases the best course of action is to ignore them. Don't feed the trolls.

Famous?

Somebody asked me
"why aint you famous?"
I told him I'm a secret agent
I'm underground way under the pavement
I'm low key out of sight like a basement
that's my choice man, that's my arrangement
he looked at me like I was braindead
but see fame is not what my aim is
besides that I am far from nameless
I've got different goals
other reasons I flow from my soul
aiming to blow is a goal too low

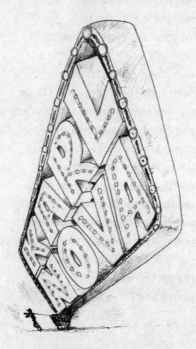

I'm on a road that's rough
but I stroll
even though my feet are cold
in world cold, but I still chose
to walk on though at times I froze
I suppose that's the way that it goes
I compose these lyrical scrolls
to expose my joys and woes
on my way, I've made friends and foes
I have clashed with those who oppose
I've fallen down but I rose
I've rocked more than a few shows
I've taken more than a few blows
had encounters that were close
but still I rep as I step
I keep crowds bouncing
with these mic checks
my vocal signature is priceless
I connect when I'm wrecking a set
with street poetry I affect
hearts and souls as the mic I bless
my lines have depth as I take a deep breath
and dive deep and release my stress
onward to my goal I press
not to impress but express
my full range and to do my best
see that to me is success
and progress part of the process
I dragged my feet and took slow steps
but now I'm here in the flesh
I've got you asking
what's next?

A lot of times when I go to perform in schools I am asked "Are you famous?" First of all if you have to ask someone if they are famous, you can be pretty sure they are not! I am known by some in certain circles but fame for me is not the reason why I do what I do and it is something I don't have or really want right now! I can thankfully go to the shop on the corner and buy some juice or whatever I want without the paparazzi chasing me!

I was in a school once and a student was convinced I knew Rihanna and there was nothing I could say to her to convince her otherwise. She kept asking me to get her autograph, hahahaha! I actually don't like too much attention apart from when I am on stage performing. I once had someone recognise me on the train and the person was going on and on and making so much noise that I was embarrassed!

I wrote this piece in response to the question of fame. So next time someone asks me "Are you famous?" I will just start reciting this verse!

Underrated

I've been told I am underrated
I'm underground and just patient
for a breakthrough I have waited
with myself I have debated
I've battled with self-hatred
by naysayers I've been slated
I thought I would never make it
dark thoughts I once contemplated
pain hit me I felt devastated
my main outlet is when creative
as an artist I felt frustrated
being celebrated is overrated
but appreciation I craved it
I thought my time was wasted
but I faced it my thoughts were basic
I could no more be so evasive
so my future I face dead on
you think I'm done, man you're dead wrong
when under pressure I press on
I don't press pause I press record
and capture even my flaws
being authentic is my cause
food for thought is my main course
served up straight from the main source
I've had mainstream dreams
but the main thing is keeping the main thing
the main thing
we all aint aiming for the same thing
we're changing, rearranging
patience

is what you need most
make sure you hold your dreams close
I inhale faith yes I breathe hope
this is real not just fancy quotes
whoa! It's peak!
I was in a valley so deep
I've heard talk is cheap
but I've paid the price to now speak
sacrifice is backing my speech
my train of thought on tracks screech
this aint a sermon but they yell PREACH!
I don't preach
I just emcee

This is a piece that goes with "Famous" A lot of times as I have been active doing music I have been told that I am underrated. I think what they mean is they think I should be more popular. I used to feel down about it because I guess I wanted recognition for what I do. I had to learn over time to not focus on all that but instead concentrate on doing what I do because I love it and because it can connect with people and benefit them in many great ways. As long as I focus on the most important things I feel happy and the funny thing is all the other things I would like to have come anyway as I do my best and stay consistent.

New Year?

It begins with a big bang
an explosion of emotions
spasms of enthusiasm
a lot of hopeful notions
most are setting goals
and making resolutions
everyone loves a fresh start
without any confusion
many are saying it's their year
denouncing everything that's negative
because out come the cynics and the sceptics
it is so repetitive
exactly a year ago
it was the same
by this time next year
it won't change
a change in the date
doesn't mean a change in you
but things can change
when your mind is renewed
it's not about what you say
it's about what you do
but adjusting your talk
can help adjust your walk too
so instead of raining on someone's parade
join in or just let people say what they say
we're all on a journey, you've heard it said
you've got to know it in your heart
as well as in your head
but anyway time keeps moving
it doesn't stand still

life is a motion picture
freeze frames give me chills
the new year is here
soon this enthusiasm will fade
and we'll be at the end of this year
bringing in another year again

I love the Christmas season. I even love that week that is in between Christmas and New Year's Day even though most times I forget what day it is! hahaha! I love counting down the clock and going crazy when midnight strikes and celebrating the arrival of the New Year. I think people really get excited at that time of the year because it gives them the idea that they can have a fresh start. It is not as easy as it sounds but I understand the idea. At this time you also have people who are critical and don't respond very well to all the excitement, I understand those people too. I wrote this poem on a New Year's Day when I was observing everything around me.

Wings

Ok it's time for take off
All baggage you have to shake off
No need for a runway to make off
Just spread your wings and stay up
How can you fly if you stay in the nest?
You've got to
give your wings a test
It can be scary I confess
You must face your fears to have success
Many things hold you down like gravity
I can feel many things grabbing me
I gain momentum as I flee
and still I rise and break free
I wonder where my wings will take me
I've gone to new heights lately
Great gusts of wind try to shake me
But I glide and soar
man it's a breeze

I glide and soar
I am so way up
I just glide and soar
Even storms help me stay up

I glide and soar
in the eye of the storm
I just glide and soar
for me it is the norm

I glide and soar
it's peaceful up here
I glide and soar
above all my fears

I just glide and soar I don't want to come down
I glide and soar above all the clouds

Ok now we are in full flight
Take a look around it is a sight
Things look different up here right?
Position affects perspective, nice!
Use your imagination
You will feel such fascination
Overcome your limitations
It will lead to celebration
spread wings gives elevation
head straight for your destination
rise above your situations
inside you will feel elation
I'm not too fond of heights
but I will get used to these flights
All my days and through dark nights
I beat fear when we have fights

I glide and soar I am so way up
I just glide and soar
Even storms help me stay up

I glide and soar in the eye of the storm
I just glide and soar for me it is the norm

I glide and soar it's peaceful up here
I glide and soar above all my fears

I just glide and soar I don't want to come down
I glide and soar above all the clouds

These are lyrics to a rap song I wrote about flying. I used it as a metaphor for rising up above challenges and difficulties. I used to not be too fond of flying in planes but now I really enjoy flying. I think the idea of being in a plane that is 30,000 feet in the air can be quite daunting. I guess I felt that way because it is not a normal thing you do every day but the more I had to fly to do shows, go on holidays and things like that, the more I felt comfortable doing it. That is just like life, when you're trying something new it can be scary but you have to try new things to know what you are good at. Imagine an eagle never stretching its wings and flying that would be so tragic.

A – Z

Almost always ambitious and attentive
Boldly building brilliantly barely bending
concentrating carefully climbing constantly
Determination defeats doubt daringly
Expecting excellence expending energy
Fighting for fantastic futures fairly
Go getters grasp golden goals
Hope helps heavy hearts hold
Intentions inside, inspiring incredibly
Jokers jest jumping joyfully
Kindness keeps kinship kindled
Laughter lifts loads, large and little
Music makes moments memorable
Never neglect news notable
Opportunities occur observe often
Perseverance produces profit
Quickly question questionable quotes

recognise remarkable routes and roads
Stories spoken shape society
Tell the truth today totally
Usually understanding's underrated
Vibrant verbalised viewpoints are venerated
Wealthy wise words won't wear out
Xavier's xylophone had silence xed out
yes youngsters yesterday's youth
Zealously and zestfully zoomed

I wrote this poem as a challenge to myself to see if I could come up with an example of alliteration using every letter of the alphabet. It ended up being a poem about things I observe in life. It is always a thrill to perform this piece and see it dawn on people what I am actually doing with the words. One thing about my style of poetry is that it is very conversational and to get the best effect you have to read them out loud.

Friends

There's nothing like having a friend that understands you
who stands with you when others just can't stand you
In a world of lies a true friend stands true
always on standby to stand up for you
it's great when you click with someone so easily
and It's not forced at all, it doesn't need to be
If life were a song you're both in harmony
You're always laughing with them so heartily
My friends are always in my heart you see
I am part of them and they are part of me
"birds of the same feather flock together"
is what I've heard said I hope we fly forever
and if in the future we part ways
I hope we meet in the sky and bask in sun rays
In my heart is where a true friend stays
because friends touch our hearts
and the fingerprint stays

There really is nothing like a good friend. Someone you can laugh with and someone who is there for you and really cares for you. As time goes on and you grow up, it even gets better if you are able to keep the friends you had from when you were young. Sometimes it isn't easy to do that but don't worry, you will always meet new people in life who can become great friends for life too.

A tale of 2 friends

Here's a story about 2 friends
from the same neighbourhood,
they called it ends
They met each other
when they were both ten
One was called Mark
the other was called Ben
Mark was really skilful at football
Ben wasn't really good at football at all
Ben was tall he was a born leader
He stood up against bullies, loved by teachers
Mark was the class clown always cracking jokes
a good kid but lost his temper when provoked
Mark and Ben they were real close
after school they hung out in each other's homes
Sometimes they talked about
what they wanted to be
Mark wanted to play in the premier league
Ben on the other hand had other dreams
He wanted to be a detective
or head of police

As they got older somehow they grew apart
that happens sometimes when you choose different paths
Mark was even more skilful with the ball on the pitch
dreaming of making it rich in the premiership
The problem is he moved with the wrong crowd
they always found him when he was in town
It was Christmas time and Mark was around
He has just been signed to Chelsea for millions of pounds

The wrong crowd he used to move with tracked him down
They got up to no good and they took Mark out
They went out partying and had a lot to drink
If only Mark slowed and took time to think
they drove around town too fast and crashed
into a police car both cars were trashed
Mark heard a voice say "You're under arrest"
It was a familiar voice, he looked up and it was Ben.

Writing poems or rap verses that are stories isn't easy at all. I hardly do it but I just had to give it a try with this tale of two friends. This is one of the times I am writing something not based on a true story, all this is purely from my imagination. Even though I just made this up, if you really think about it, this story could actually be true.

The amazing discovery

I can only be myself
and honestly I don't want to be anyone else
it's ok to be you knowing that is wealth
before I knew this I was stuck in my shell
looking at me now it would be hard to tell
but my story is deeper than an old well
these words I've found
within me they swelled
until I burst like a balloon and started to tell
all these tales with verses and lyrics
the truth is being yourself is terrific
everyone has a talent in some way you're gifted
discovering yourself is like finding a magic ticket
that will take you on a journey, a magical ride
Let your imagination come alive as you glide
it begins in your heart and your mind
when you discover being you is alright!

Being yourself is the best thing to be. Sometimes it takes a while to discover this fact and truly believe this. Even people who are grown up struggle with this. Everyone is unique and different and that is ok, in fact is it the best thing in the world. The more you grow, the more you learn about yourself and what you can do. It is an amazing discovery when you find out what you can do.

The man who wanted to dance

There once was a man from France
who wanted to learn how to dance
He had 2 left feet
and he danced off beat
so he never really stood a chance.

A Limerick is a certain kind of poetry done in a certain kind of style. It is normally short and funny. The name limerick is generally taken to be a reference to the City or County of Limerick in Ireland. I made this one up on the spot off the top of my head when I visited a school to show an example of this type of poetry. Everyone laughed and I thought to myself "This actually isn't that bad, I am going to add it to my book" and here we are.

The City of my birth

I spy with my London eye
Big Ben telling the time
as these thoughts like the River Thames
flow through my mind
Thoughts of love for my city
Like tube trains move quickly
Although unlike them
there's no delay, swiftly
like red buses that move through the streets
Like the blood pumping through my veins
as my heart beats
I feel a rush of love for the city of my birth
I might be biased, it's one of the greatest on earth
I stand still on Westminster bridge watching the movement
of different people moving around I am grooving
to music pumping in my headphones, I crack a smile
London is my playground and I am its child.

I love London. I was born in Belsize Park which is in North West London. I really do believe London is one of the greatest cities on earth. I am always discovering new things and new places in this city I was born in. I haven't explored every single place in London yet and that actually makes living here exciting. You just never know what you are going to find out next in the city of my birth.

For you

I have your smile
when I look in the mirror I see you
I have your laugh
So when I chuckle I hear you
I have your humour
when I'm sharing jokes I owe it to you
You taught me to be kind
You and I know it's true
You cook the best rice and chicken on the planet!
You made me like broccoli normally I can't stand it
Your voice is like the music of my favourite song
No one else sounds like you so loving and warm
When I was young, I was separated from you for very long
those were hard times for me but somehow I was strong
because of you I learnt to write letters and buy the right stamps
So I could send bright messages that glowed like lamps
We reconnected when I was fully grown
Deep inside I always knew I would come home
I love you mum we've both come a long way
I don't have to wait to show you on Mother's Day.

I don't even have to tell you I love my mother. She is just simply the best! We were indeed separated for a long time when I was seven years old. I had to go and live with my father far away in Lagos, Nigeria. I was there for a long time but kept in touch by writing letters and talking to her on the phone. We reconnected when I was all grown up. I had to write a poem for her. When she reads this she will be surprised because I didn't tell her I would!

The living book

I know this might seem strange
but hear me out
Listen closely you'll know what I'm talking about
A brand new book I received as a gift
There was something special about this
normally I'm not one to care about books
I'm sure some of you are giving me funny looks
this book seemed magical the cover was colourful
I was fascinated because it looked wonderful
I held it in my hands and looked at it for ages
then I opened it and gazed at the pages
the words seemed to jump out and dance around
I could feel a rhythm though I heard no sound
I snapped the book shut, I could feel my heart pound
because it was so weird and so profound
I looked at the cover filled with colours loud
The book was called "Rhythm And Poetry"
you're reading it now.

Sometimes a book can feel like it is alive, especially when it sparks up your imagination. I always tell people who find reading boring that it is only that way to them because they haven't found the book that really interests them. When you do find a book that captures your imagination, it feels like the book is alive. I hope reading my book does that for you. If it doesn't, there is always a book out there for you that will feel like it is alive in your hands when you read it.

I wrote these words

I wrote these words to inspire you
to lift you to a higher view
and when life stresses you and tires you
Let these words refresh you
Speak them out loud when life tests you
Allow them to paint a smile on your face
and tickle your funny bone
Share them with your friends or take them in all alone
They come from my experience also imagination
I'm passing on this inspiration
with this unique poetic communication
that will have you caught up in fascination
I want these words to paint pictures in your mind
So you can see them clearly even when you close your eyes
like a memory of a sunrise
Poetry is like photography capturing sights
capturing life with words that I arrange
in a pattern full of rhythm that will stimulate your brain

This is one of the last poems I wrote for this collection that you are reading. It simply states what I hope reading this does for you. I never dreamed of writing a book but here I am. It was difficult writing this poem because I knew I needed one more for the book but didn't know what to write. I just had the idea of speaking directly to you the reader. Thanks again for reading this. I hope you enjoyed everything.

My First rap verse ever

He's tall and he's skinny
and he's here to stay
his name is Fido Dido
you know anyway
he's cool, he's great
and a nice type of guy
and he says 7up
is the one you gotta buy
when you take a sip
and it goes down your throat
it's even better
than being on a pleasure boat
whenever you're thirsty
7up is near
which goes to show
the difference is clear

I wasn't going to include this verse in this collection because I don't think it is very good at all but this is in fact the very first rap verse I ever wrote. I was about 14 years old when I wrote this and I am amazed I still remember it. You might be wondering, why in the world did I choose to write about a soft drink of all things. Well there is a reason.

I remember seeing in a magazine I was reading that there was a competition to get free tickets to see Michael Jackson in concert. All you had to do was write a rap about Coca-Cola and you could be the winner. I was happy because I thought to myself "that is easy" but when I checked the closing date for entries, I found out that I had missed my chance.

I decided to write about 7up because I thought if 7up did a similar kind of competition I would be ready. Imagine that, my motivation to write was to win something, what if I never saw any competition in a magazine? Fido Dido was the 7up advert mascot at the time and he used to have lots of cool adverts. You can actually search for them on YouTube right now and watch them; they were so creative and fun.

I don't think this piece is good but it is significant to me because it is the very first time I wrote anything in that way. Imagine if I had never written it, would I be writing a book today? Would I be writing songs and poems? I think I would be but who knows? We all have to start from somewhere and that was my starting point.

Acknowledgements

I would like to thank God, The Creator of all things and the one who blessed me with the ability and inspiration to create. I would like to thank my mother who put books in my hands from when I was a child. Thank you so much for setting me on the path I am on because you made me fall in love with words that painted pictures on the canvas of my imagination. I can now place a book I wrote in your hands. I would like to thank my father for helping me to be a writer and drilling me with writing exercises when I was very young. I would like thank Breis who showed me how to take this poetic gift into classrooms and positively impact young people, the next generation, and the future.